STORIES FOR YOUNG

OUR MEXICAN ANCESTORS

VOLUME ONE

STORIES FOR YOUNG READERS

OUR MEXICAN ANCESTORS
—VOLUME ONE—

Writer and Educational Consultant
Dr. D. Jeanne Callihan
Trinity University

Principal Researcher
Samuel P. Nesmith
The University of Texas
Institute of Texan Cultures at San Antonio

The University of Texas
Institute
of Texan
Cultures
at San Antonio
1981

Jack R. Maguire, Executive Director
Pat Maguire, Director of Publications and
Coordinator of Programs

Barbara Shimkus, Designer
Thom Ricks, Illustrator

Library of Congress Catalog Card Number 78-057798
International Standard Book Number 0-933164-38-6

This publication was made possible by grants from
The Brown Foundation, The Levi Strauss Foundation,
The Houston Endowment, Incorporated,
The Institute of Texan Cultures Associates and
the Mexican Market of the Texas Folklife Festival.

CONTENTS

PREFACE

The names, places and dates in the following stories are true. Only the conversation in some stories is make-believe because the words actually spoken were not usually written down. When they were, the writings were often lost or destroyed later. In these stories, the conversations are only what might have been said at the time.

The stories in this book are written for children. If you are in kindergarten, first or second grade, you will enjoy them as they are read to you. If you are in the third grade or above, you can read them for yourself. Pronunciation aids for proper names are given within parentheses in the fewest possible sounds, so you can use them by yourself. They give the way that names are pronounced in Texas today.

You will find some stories more interesting than others. Not all have a happy ending. In real life, not everyone lives "happily ever after." These are real people. Sometimes people are misunderstood and are taken advantage of by others. Sometimes this happens when two people or two groups of people are different, when they look different or when they think, feel or do things in a different way. The more we try to understand someone else, the better we understand ourselves. That is the challenge of these stories – and of life itself.

MEET THE MEXICAN TEXANS

When we think of Texas today, we think of a big and beautiful state. We think of farms and ranches and busy cities. We think of oil wells, waterways and many kinds of factories. And most of all, we think of many people, all kinds of people, who make their homes in Texas.

Where did all the people come from? How did they help Texas to become a great state? These questions can best be answered by taking a close look at some interesting facts and a few stories about some of the people who came to live in Texas many years ago. In this book, we will talk about people who came to Texas from Mexico and who are known as Mexican Texans.

What is a Mexican Texan?

A Mexican Texan is a person who lives in Texas and who was born in a family of Mexican heritage. This can mean that someone in his or her family, like a parent or grandparent

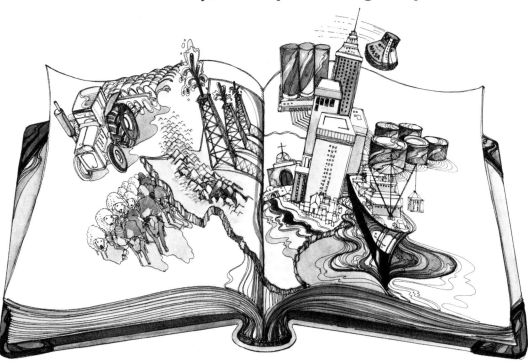

or even a great-great-great grandparent, belonged to one of the native Indian tribes which once lived in Mexico. This would be called Mexican Indian heritage.

Another way to be a Mexican Texan is to have a Spanish heritage. This would be a

person who has a parent or grandparent or great-great-great grandparent who once came from Spain to live in Mexico. And, of course, a person might have a heritage from both of these sources.

When a person is born and grows up in a certain country, he learns to like and to do the things that the adults do there. He has special holidays to celebrate. He may have a special costume to wear or special foods to eat. There may even be a special language to learn and special ways of saying things or thinking about things. All of these special ways of doing and saying and thinking are called customs and traditions. Many of these are still seen today and enjoyed by all Texans, not just by those with Mexican heritage.

Many Mexicans have last names, or sur-
names, which are Spanish, such as Gonzalez
or Padilla or Rodriguez. But some do not. A
Mexican woman may not have a Spanish
surname if she marries a man from a non-
Mexican family. Her children, having the same
last name as their father, may not have a

Spanish surname either. Many Mexicans speak Spanish, but some do not. Many Mexicans have dark hair and eyes, but some do not. A person can tell about his or her heritage only after knowing about his or her parents, their parents and their parents from long ago.

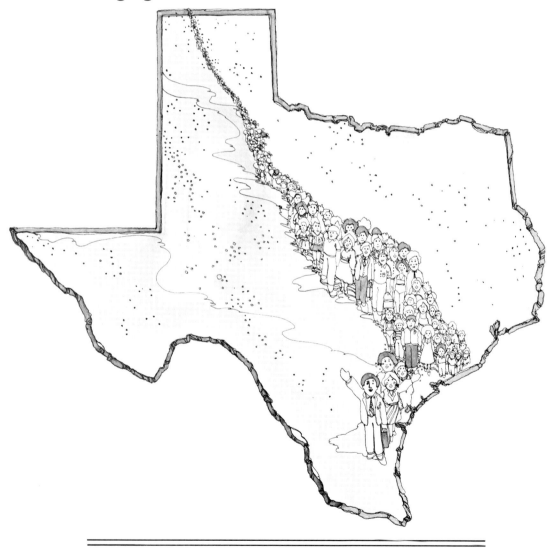

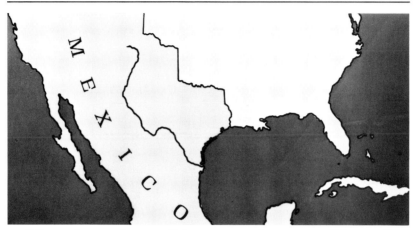

How long have Mexicans been in Texas?

Mexicans have been in this part of the country for so long that it is hard to think of a time when they were not here. In fact, Texas was really a part of Mexico for over 300 years. During this time (1519-1836), when a Mexican came to Texas, he really was going to just another part of Mexico.

Are there many Mexicans in Texas?

Yes, there are many Mexicans in Texas. There have been Mexicans in Texas for a long time. Today, more than one person out of every five could be called a Mexican Texan. If the nearly three million people who are of Mexican heritage stood in one long line, the line would reach all across Texas from the tip to the top!

The Mexicans have helped make Texas what it is today. Since some of the Mexicans came from Indian peoples and some came from Spanish peoples, let us look at some stories about each of these.

THE AZTECS AND THE EAGLE

Once upon a time, many years ago, a group of people called the Aztec Indians lived in the country we now call Mexico. They were a powerful tribe which liked to fight other people. They traveled from place to place making war on weaker tribes and taking what they wanted.

The Aztecs believed that there were many gods and that these gods could speak to them by sending messages to their leaders. One day their leaders received a special message from their gods. The gods told the leaders that it was time to find a new home. They were told to search until they found an eagle sitting on a cactus eating a snake. That would be the place where they should build their capital city.

The Aztecs spent many, many years searching. One day, when they were traveling in the Valley of Mexico, they came upon an eagle sitting on a cactus with a snake in his beak, just as they had been told they would many, many years before. Here, at last, they had found the sign for which they had been looking. But there was one problem. The cactus on which the eagle was sitting was growing on a small island right in the middle of a lake! How could they build a city in the middle of a lake? What should they do now?

The leaders and the people talked it over. They all prayed to their gods and asked what they should do. But their gods did not answer.

The people received no new information, and the leaders received no new message. So they decided to go ahead and build their capital city on the island, right in the middle of the lake.

They named their capital Tenochtitlan (Tĕ nōch´ tĭt lăn´). The city (started in 1324) became one of the most beautiful and richest cities in that part of the world. It grew so large that it covered the island and the land around the lake in the Valley of Mexico. Today we know this capital by the name of Mexico City. The eagle sitting on a cactus with a snake in his beak became a very special symbol. And that symbol, pictured above on the 1823-1910 flag of Mexico, is still used, although the eagle on today's flag looks a little different.

Cortés – The Conqueror from Spain

We learned earlier that many Mexicans are of Indian descent. Many others have some Spanish heritage, too. The story of how the Spaniards came to Mexico and what they did there is a very interesting story. It is best told in three short stories: *The Road to the Aztec Capital, Tenochtitlan: The Golden City* and *Cortés Returns to Conquer*. It will be more fun to read them in order.

The Road to the Aztec Capital

The first Spaniards came to Mexico over 400 years ago. Their leader was an explorer named Hernando Cortés (Cŏr tĕz′), who came to look for riches. Cortés and a few hundred other soldiers from Spain got 11 ships together to

form a small fleet. They sailed for many days and finally landed in Mexico (in 1519).

Mexican Indians were living at the place where Cortés landed. They had never seen Spanish soldiers dressed in iron armor and carrying guns and cannons. Also, they had never before seen horses. They thought the horse with his rider was all one big monster! They were afraid and did not want them to land. When the Spaniards did land, a battle

began. The Indians wore jackets of padded cloth and carried wooden shields. They fought with stone-tipped arrows and stone-edged axes. They were no match for well-armed Spaniards and soon gave up the fight. In this battle, Cortés was the winner, the conqueror.

After the battle, the Indians brought presents for Cortés and his men: fish, birds, fruits, dogs, ducks and golden ornaments. They also gave them women slaves to do their work. One of the women was an intelligent young Indian princess who had been sold into slavery by her parents. She spoke several Indian languages, including that of the Aztecs. She was used as an interpreter to help Cortés under-

stand the Indian languages. The Spanish named her Doña Marina. Many Indians, however, called her *Malinche* and considered her a traitor because she helped the Spaniards.

After a time, Cortés, his servants and the soldiers boarded their ships again. They sailed along the coast of Mexico looking for a rich city to conquer. They landed near what is now called Veracruz. Here they met the local

Indians, members of the powerful Aztec nation. These Indians liked Cortés, and gifts were exchanged.

With the help of Doña Marina, Cortés sent a message to the great Aztec leader,

Montezuma (Mŏn tĕ sū´mǎh), and asked to meet with him. After several days, Montezuma sent back gifts of gold and precious stones, but he said "no" to a meeting. Cortés was sure there must be much more gold and treasure in Montezuma's capital city of Tenochtitlan. He wanted to capture the city and take all the riches for himself.

Some of Cortés's men did not want to fight any more and wished to go home. They secretly planned to steal a ship and sail for Spain without permission. But Cortés discovered their plan and sank their ships. Now no one could go home. There was no choice but to go on to the Aztec capital.

It took a long time to travel the distance to the capital city. The Spanish soldiers fought many battles along the way and conquered many Indian cities. Cortés heard from many people that Montezuma was a powerful emperor who ruled all the land around the city and forced his people to give him gifts. They

brought gifts of gold and silver, colorful feathers and precious jewels. They also had to bring large numbers of men and women to be killed as sacrifices to the Aztec gods.

As Cortés and his army drew closer to the city, Montezuma remembered an old, old story. It told of a fair-skinned, light-haired god named Quetzalcoatl (Kĕtz'ăl cō wătl'). This god had a beard like the Spaniards and had lived with the Aztecs a long time ago. He had taught them many things, such as how to grow crops, build better buildings and make things of metal. When he had gone away, he promised the Aztecs he would return someday to visit his people. Montezuma thought Cortés was this god returning to them. He welcomed Cortés and his men into the city of Tenochtitlan. They were given food and gifts and treated as gods.

Tenochtitlan: The Golden City

The Spaniards discovered that the stories they had heard about the Aztecs were true. Montezuma had gold and riches of many kinds. They also learned that the Aztecs wor-

shiped many gods and made human sacrifices to them. These human sacrifices were men and women who were killed to make the gods happy. The Spaniards thought this was wrong and tried to make them stop. But the Aztecs continued to worship in this way.

Gradually, the Spaniards and the Aztecs became less afraid of each other. Montezuma even agreed to let Cortés visit him at his palace to show that they were friends. At the end of

the visit, Cortés asked Montezuma to return with him to the house where he and his soldiers were staying. When Montezuma arrived, he was taken prisoner. Although he was treated kindly, he was never allowed to return to his own palace again. Cortés did not want the Aztecs to know that Montezuma was being held prisoner. He thought they might stop bringing food and gifts to their emperor. For that reason, Montezuma's family and friends were allowed to visit him whenever they wished.

A strange friendship grew between Montezuma and Cortés. They exchanged many gifts and even went hunting together. Cortés allowed Montezuma to continue to visit the temple to worship his gods. Montezuma then allowed the Spaniards to put up a cross and a statue of the Virgin Mary in a corner of the great Aztec temple. This act made Montezuma's people very angry. They decided

to drive the Spaniards from their city.

During this time, Cortés heard that other Spanish ships had landed on the coast. He took some of his men and went to investigate. The Spaniards who had just arrived came to make Cortés their prisoner and take the Aztec gold for themselves. Cortés conquered the new arrivals, and they agreed to join his army. Then messengers arrived from Tenochtitlan. The soldiers who had stayed in the city to guard Montezuma were in trouble. The Aztecs had continued with their plan to drive the Spaniards out of the city. They had burned part of the building where the emperor was being held. Many of the Spaniards had been killed or wounded. They needed help. Cortés took his soldiers and some Indians who wanted to help and returned to Tenochtitlan.

It was quiet when Cortés and his army arrived in the city to join his other men. The next day, the Aztecs attacked more fiercely than before with stones, arrows and loud cries. The battle lasted all day, most of the night and for many days to follow. There were so many Aztecs that when one was killed, several others took his place in battle. Soon every Spanish soldier was wounded.

Cortés now knew that he could not win and wanted to leave the city with his men. He asked Montezuma to speak to his people and ask them to let the Spaniards go without more fighting. The Aztecs listened while Montezuma spoke to them from the roof of a tall building. After he finished, they told him they had chosen another emperor. They said they would fight until every Spaniard was dead. Then they showered the roof top where he stood with arrows and stones. One of the stones hit Montezuma on the head. He was led downstairs, and three days later he died. With Montezuma dead, the Spaniards were really in trouble. There were angry Aztecs all around, and no one to help them.

The Spaniards decided to escape from the city at night. Since the city was built on an island with water all around it, their escape was very difficult. The Aztecs had destroyed all the bridges on the roads connecting the island with the shores. There were no boats for the soldiers to use, and it was too far to swim to the other side. The Spaniards worked quickly and built a small, portable wooden bridge which they could carry along with them and use in place of the ruined ones.

When it was dark, they slipped quietly out to the first crossing and set their bridge in place. As they crossed, they were suddenly attacked from all sides by the Aztecs. The Spaniards tried to pick up the bridge, but it would not move – it was stuck! They fought their way down the roadway to the next crossing. But they had no bridge to fill the gap and could not go forward. The Aztecs were on both sides of them and behind them, and they could not go

backward. The battle was long and bloody. Hundreds and hundreds of people, both Aztecs and Spaniards, were killed. Soon the bodies of dead men and horses which fell into the water made another kind of bridge. Some used this bridge, and others tried to swim. One man used his spear as a pole and tried to vault across the water. The battle lasted all night.

By morning, most of the Spanish soldiers had been killed or captured. All of those left were badly wounded. All of their guns and

cannons were gone. They had lost the gold and treasures which they had taken from the Aztecs. It had been a terrible night, a night of sorrow and pain and death. So it was called the *noche triste*, which means the sad night. It was the night they had been driven out of Tenochtitlan, the golden city of the Aztecs.

Cortés Returns to Conquer

Cortés and a few of his men had escaped from the city, but there were still many Aztecs all around them. They had to fight for many weeks before they finally reached the coast.

There Cortés found other ships from Spain with men and supplies. Some of them had not come as friends, but Cortés soon had them on his side. It was not long before he had built up another army. Then he made two important decisions. He decided to allow his old soldiers who wanted to go home to do so. And, he decided to go back to Tenochtitlan and conquer the city.

For months he trained the new soldiers and sailors into a fighting team. Some of the men were ship builders and built ships Cortés could use in battle. The ships were a special kind that he could take apart like blocks, move across the land and then put back together again very quickly. These were needed to help the men cross the lake to the city.

Cortés and his men and boats were finally ready. They began the trip to the Aztec city of Tenochtitlan. Many Indian cities were con-

quered along the way. At last they reached the edge of the lake which surrounded the city. They took the parts of the boats to a field nearby and put them together. Then they dug a deep ditch from the boats to the lake. Now Cortés was ready to return to the city and battle the Aztecs again.

The Spaniards launched their ships and began their attack on the city. This time there was no welcome for the Spaniards. The Aztecs did not want them back. Day after day they fought each other in and around the city. It took 75 days and thousands of lives for the Spaniards to conquer the city. By the time they took the city, most of the buildings were torn down or burned. The new emperor finally surrendered, and all of the Aztecs who were still alive became slaves. Cortés and his soldiers branded the slaves with hot irons in the same way people brand cattle.

The Aztecs who had once been proud and strong were now hungry and sick. The city smelled terrible from the odor of dead bodies that had not been buried. The gold and treasures that were once in the city were nowhere to be found. The great Aztec nation had been destroyed. The Spanish soldiers began to rule the conquered nation. They would rule there for about 300 years. During this time, many Spaniards married Indians. From these families came many of the Mexicans who are in Texas today.

THE EARLY SETTLERS
OF TEXAS

For over a hundred years after Cortés had conquered the Aztecs, the Spaniards were too busy with their new land to think about Texas. Their ships did some exploring along the Texas coast but did not stay long.

The Spaniards were not interested in settling Texas until they heard the French were living there. The Spanish and French did not like each other. The Spaniards were afraid the French might take over Texas, and so they sent out men to look for them. After looking for several years, they found the French fort (1689). It had been burned, and the French had been killed by the Indians.

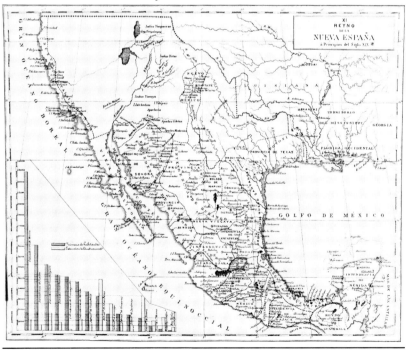

After this, the Spaniards decided they would have to build towns, missions and forts in Texas. These would keep other Frenchmen from coming to Texas and building homes.

The Spanish first sent priests and soldiers to settle in the unknown land. Later, farmers and ranchers and other settlers followed. On these early journeys to Texas, the people in charge were usually Spaniards, and most of the others were Mexicans. The following stories are about some of the Mexicans who came to Texas as early settlers.

ESPINOSA AND SAN ANTONIO

In the Mexican state of Coahuila (Cō ăh we'lă) in a small town now called Guerrero (Gŭh'rer' rōw), a mission had been built. In the early 1700's, this mission of San Juan Bautista del Río Grande received a new priest. His name was Fray Isidro Felix de Espinosa (Ĕs'pĕn nō' să). He worked hard at the mission carrying out his duties.

One of the most important things Espinosa did happened in 1709. He and some soldiers came to a beautiful part of Texas. They camped near some springs of water where there were friendly Indians. The springs were later called San Pedro Springs. A mission and a fort were built in the area nine years later, and a town called San Antonio grew up around it. This was the first Spanish town in what was then Texas.

THE FIRST SCHOOLS IN TEXAS

The first schools in Texas were those started for Indians by the missions or churches. In 1746, a school was started that was not a part of a mission. A man named Don Cristobal de los Santos Coy helped to set it up at San Antonio. The government gave the land on which to build it, the church built the building, and the people who lived there took care of it.

Another school was started in San Antonio (in 1789). A man from Saltillo named Don José Francisco de la Mata began it.

Later another school was opened in San Antonio (in 1811), and for ten years children studied there. Juan Zambrano started the school for 70 pupils. Each pupil had to pay whatever his father could send. If the parents had no money, they paid with food, clothing or other goods. The teacher was paid $30 a month. There was a special man called a

regidor who punished the pupils when they did not do what the teacher asked.

Five years after Zambrano's school closed, another school opened in San Antonio (1826). Two years later, the governor bought charts, maps, Catholic books and other supplies with tax money. He gave them to the school. This was the first time school children in Texas had free textbooks to use. That same year (1828) a law was passed which allowed the children in Texas to have "free public primary school."

Schools were very expensive. It took money to pay the teachers, buy books and care for the buildings. Texans did not have a lot of money. When the money ran out, many schools had to close. Some schools closed because pupils did not want to go any longer. Some children had to help their families work.

TWO TEXAS TOWNS

Two towns in Texas were started, or established, by two wealthy cattle ranchers from Mexico. One of these cattlemen, José Vásquez Borrego (Bō rāy'gō), owned ranches on both sides of the Río Grande. The Mexican governor of the area gave Borrego some more land east of the river on which to establish a town. He built the town of Dolores (in 1750), south of where Laredo is now located. When there was fighting between the Spanish and the Mexicans, the Borrego families were driven off the land but later returned. The little town of Dolores had a fort, church, school and several houses. A century later, unfriendly Indians destroyed the town. Now there are only a few stone walls left.

Another rancher, Tomás Sanchez (Sǎn´ chěz), received a grant of land (in 1755). The Villa de Laredo was built on the east bank of the Río Grande, 30 miles from Dolores. Since it was on a busy road, it grew and grew. Sanchez became the mayor and served until his death. Laredo is still a very important city.

YBARBO AND NACOGDOCHES

The capital of Texas was once at Los Adaes, which is now a part of Louisiana. This was the town where Antonio Gil Ybarbo (Ē băr′bo) was born and grew up. His parents had come from Spain to Los Adaes to make their home.

When Ybarbo grew up, the government moved the capital to San Antonio. They also closed the fort at Los Adaes and made all the people move. The people had to leave their homes and move to farmlands near San Antonio. The journey was very long and very hard. Many people died on the trip. They were not happy with the new land. Ybarbo asked the Spanish government to let them go back to their old homes. The answer was "no," but they were allowed to move to land near the Trinity River which grew better crops than their land in San Antonio. There they built a town called Bucareli (Boo′căh rāy′lēē). It is said that Ybarbo took with him cottonseed and sheep. He took a Negro weaver to teach the people how to make cloth.

The settlers had problems in growing food and getting supplies. Also, the Comanche Indians began to bother them. They began to destroy property and take things that did not belong to them. Ybarbo and the other settlers wanted more guns and bullets to fight the Indians. They could not get any. Then a very

bad flood came and destroyed almost everything. The families had to leave.

Ybarbo led the families to a deserted mission called Nacogdoches in 1779. Ybarbo and the men built a town around the mission and named the town Nacogdoches. He died at his ranch near there in 1809.

LEAL AND THE MUSTANGS

Antonio Leal (Lāy ăhl´) was born in San Antonio. He lived a quiet life until he met an Irish trader named Philip Nolan (in 1790).

The two men captured wild horses called mustangs. They kept them on Leal's large ranch where the town of San Augustine now stands. Then they would take the horses to Louisiana and sell them.

The Spanish government did not like this. They thought the two men were selling horses to the Anglo Americans. The Anglo Americans were the citizens of the United States. The Spaniards were afraid the Anglo Americans might want to take Texas away from them. They also thought Leal and Nolan were drawing maps of the Spanish lands to give to the enemy, the Anglo Americans. So the government decided to stop them.

The government sent soldiers to capture Nolan the next time he came to catch mustangs. But Nolan would not give up, and a fight began. During the battle, Nolan was killed, and all of his men were captured.

The soldiers then went on to the ranch and arrested Leal and his wife. They were put into prison in San Antonio. There was a long, famous trial. When it was over, the Leals were freed from jail, but the government would not let them stay near the Louisiana border. They had to leave their ranch and move to San Antonio where the government could keep an eye on them. They were no longer allowed to capture mustangs.

DOÑA MARÍA — THE BLACK-HAIRED BEAUTY ON THE WHITE STALLION

Of all the ranchers in early Texas, one of the most interesting was a woman named Doña María del Carmen Calvillo (Că ve´yo).

Doña María was born in 1765, and she lived to be nearly 100 years old. Her father had come from the Canary Islands and settled on a large tract of land in Texas near Paso de las Mujeres (Crossing of the Women). This was an important ford, a place on the San Antonio River near Floresville where people could wade across the river.

Doña María grew up there, and when she was older, she married Gavino Delgado. When her father died, he left her all his land. It was called El Rancho de las Cabras – The Ranch of the Goats. It had once been owned by the Mission Espada in San Antonio. Doña María was very proud of her ranch.

For awhile, Doña María was very happy. She had a husband and two lovely children, a big house with stone walls 12 feet high, and many goats and cattle on her land. Then she and her husband became unhappy living together, and she asked him to leave the ranch. He left, thinking that she would find it impossible to get along without him. "She will soon ask me to come back," he thought. "Only a man can look after a ranch this big and busy."

But Doña María was a very unusual woman for her time, and she had a mind of her own. She decided to manage the ranch all by herself. There were men and their families on the ranch to help her, and she could tell them what to do.

Doña María spent many hours going all over the ranch to see that her orders were carried out exactly as she had given them. She rode a large white horse called a stallion. Often she could be seen galloping across the countryside on her white stallion with her long black hair flying in the wind. She rode like a man, she dressed like a man, and she could shoot and rope like a man.

Under her care, the ranch got bigger and better. There were 1,500 head of cattle, 500 goats and sheep, and many horses, donkeys and other farm animals. They had a large irrigation system with special ditches in order to carry water to the crops. There was a sugar mill on the ranch and a granary for storing food for the winter. Doña María had 20 families living on the ranch who could do many things. Some worked as carpenters, while others worked as blacksmiths, tailors or brick makers.

Many neighboring ranches had trouble with the Indians who would steal or kill the ani-

mals, burn the barns and houses, and, sometimes, injure the people. One day a large band of Indians came onto Doña María's ranch. She sent all her families into her big house for safety, and she rode out on her white stallion all alone to meet them.

She tied a white handkerchief to her gun, showing she came in peace. The Indian chief tied a white cloth to his spear and met her in the middle of the field. They shook hands to show they wanted to be friends. Doña María waved to her cowboys, and six of them rode quickly to her side. She told them to go back and bring 20 cows as a gift for the Indians. The Indians killed six cows immediately and from

each one, cut out a big chunk of meat about 12 inches square. They built a fire. They roasted the meat with the hide still on it and ate it. Doña María and the cowboys returned to the big house. The Indians spent the night in the field, and the next morning they rode peacefully away, taking the remaining cows with them. They never destroyed the ranch property or harmed the families. In later years, whenever the Indians wanted cattle or grain, they would come to the ranch, and Doña María would give them what they wanted.

Doña María had two more children, but

she did not marry again. She must have loved these children very much for when she died, she left all her land to her last two children. And they remembered her as the "black-haired beauty who rode the white stallion" on El Rancho de las Cabras.

FIGHTERS FOR INDEPENDENCE

In the early 1800's, after Texas had gained more settlers, the people began to want freedom. They were tired of the Spanish government telling them what to do. They

wanted to do things their way. They wanted to be "independent." The next stories are about people who lived and did important things during this time.

At this time, remember, Texas was still a part of Mexico. Mexico was ruled by Spain, and the Mexican people did not like that. Spain sent Spaniards all the way across the Atlantic Ocean in order to be heads of the government, commanders over the soldiers and leaders of the churches.

The Spaniards born in Mexico were called *criollos* (krēē ō′yōs). They were not allowed to be heads or commanders or rulers of anything. The Spaniards from Spain, called *peninsulares* (pĕ nĭn sŏŏ lär′rāys), thought the *criollos* were not very intelligent and not as good as they were. They thought the same thing about the

Indians in Mexico. Both groups were allowed only to do the hard work and jobs that the *peninsulares* did not want to do. This was also true for *mestizos* (mĕss tēe′zōs), the children of Spaniards who had married Indians.

By 1810, the *criollos* and Indians and *mestizos* were tired of being told what to do. They were tired of never getting to help plan anything or make decisions. They wanted their freedom and their independence from Spain and the *peninsulares*.

Father Miguel Hidalgo (Ĕ dăhl′go) was a priest who decided to help. He began to hold secret meetings with the *criollos* and *mestizos*

who wanted independence. Meetings were
held in many cities in Mexico. At the meetings,
the men made plans to fight against the
peninsulares until the *peninsulares* left all parts

of Mexico, including Texas. When a group of people fight for their independence from another country, it is called a "revolution." Father Hidalgo started the Mexican Revolution against Spain.

After making a speech for independence, Father Hidalgo led an army of *criollos*,

mestizos and Indians against the Spanish. Although they won several battles, Hidalgo's army was defeated. Hidalgo tried to escape through Texas to the United States but was captured and shot. His death did not stop his followers from wanting their freedom.

A man named Juan Bautista de las Casas (Căh´ sas) was commander of the Spanish troops in San Antonio. But he liked Hidalgo's ideas about freedom. He had his troops arrest the governor, Manuel Salcedo, and his assistant, the lieutenant governor. Las Casas made himself the new governor, but the people in San Antonio did not like the way he governed.

One of the men who did not like las Casas was Juan Manuel Zambrano (Zăm brăn´ no). He organized a group of men, and in the middle of the night, they took las Casas prisoner. After a short trial, las Casas was executed. Zambrano let Governor Salcedo and his men go free and made Salcedo governor again. As before, the Spanish controlled Texas.

INDEPENDENCE – FOR A SHORT TIME

One of the Mexicans who wanted Mexico to be free from Spain was José Bernardo Maximiliano Gutiérrez de Lara (Gōō tēē ĕr´ rĕs). He was one of Hidalgo's followers who had managed to escape across the Mexican border. He had gone to Louisiana in the United States. He wanted very much to go back to Texas in Mexico and help the people get their freedom from the Spanish rulers.

Gutiérrez put together an army. Some of the men were Mexicans who had been forced to leave Mexico because they had fought the Spanish. Some were Indians. Other men were Anglo Americans from the United States who wanted to help. Still others just thought it would be exciting to fight in a war.

When the army was ready (late 1812), Gutiérrez and his men crossed the Sabine River into Texas. They had no problems in taking over the town of Nacogdoches. Next, they captured Goliad. Then (April 1813), they captured San Antonio, which was the capital of Texas.

The Spanish governor and his staff were put into prison. On April 6, 1813, Gutiérrez proclaimed, "Now Mexico is free from Spain. Mexico is now a new, independent country – a republic. And Texas will be a state in the new Republic of Mexico." This was the first "Declaration of Independence" for Texas. This meant there was no more Spanish control in the Mexican state of Texas.

But this did not mean there was peace. Some of the Mexicans from San Antonio who were with Gutiérrez did not like the Spanish governor. The governor had been the cause of injury or death to many of their friends and relatives. One day, without telling Gutiérrez, they took the governor and his staff from prison. They told him they were going to set him and his men free. Instead, they took them outside of town and killed them in a brutal way.

When news of these murders reached the other soldiers in Gutiérrez' army, many did not think this should have happened. Some of the Anglo Americans who did not like it returned to the United States. Many of the soldiers who stayed blamed Gutiérrez for the brutal murders. They no longer trusted him or wanted to follow him. After four months of facing these problems, Gutiérrez decided to give up his command. He, too, left Texas and went back to Louisiana.

When Gutiérrez left, Alvarez de Toledo (Tō lāy' dō) took over as commander of the army. He had very little experience leading men in battle. He had much to learn.

Spain had not forgotten Texas and sent a large Spanish army to recapture San Antonio. They decided to set a trap for Toledo's army. The soldiers hid in the trees near the Medina River. Toledo did not see the hidden soldiers and led his men into the Spanish trap. Toledo's army was badly defeated. Almost all of his men were either killed or taken prisoner. The Spanish, who had won the battle, took over and again ruled Mexico. Texas was no longer an independent state in the Republic of Mexico. All the land was under Spanish rule once more.

INDEPENDENCE AT LAST— MEXICO IS FREE

Mexicans continued to fight the Spanish. But the fighting was scattered and not all in one place. These small battles helped to make Mexico stronger and Spanish rule weaker.

Several men gave important help during this time. José Félix Trespalacios (Trāce pǎ lǎ′ sēē ōs′) had been put in prison twice because he had led some of the fighting against Spain.

Then he joined Dr. James Long, who was also fighting for Mexican independence. They captured Goliad (also called La Bahía) from the Spaniards. Long sent him and another man, Ben Milam, to Mexico to ask for help. They were told to visit the head of the Spanish army, Colonel Agustín de Iturbide (Ē to͝or bē´day), to see if he would join them.

Before they got there, Trespalacios and Milam were captured and put into prison. But Colonel Iturbide liked the idea after he heard about it. He thought he might have more power if he helped the Mexicans gain their independence. So the people's army of Mexico and the royal Spanish army under Iturbide joined forces. They signed a paper called the "Plan of Iguala" which joined the two armies together as equals. This is important because whoever controlled the army controlled the whole country.

The last Spanish governor of Texas, Antonio Martinez, was in power when the Plan of Iguala was signed. He had been one of the best Texas governors because he was honest and helpful. But when he saw the plan joining the two armies, he quit being governor. He "resigned." The Spanish accepted the Plan of Iguala, and Mexico finally gained her independence from Spain in 1821.

Iturbide went to Mexico City and made himself the first emperor of Mexico. Iturbide freed Trespalacios and Milam, who were still in prison. The new emperor was grateful for their help and made Trespalacios a colonel in the army and then governor of Texas.

COAHUILA Y TEJAS – A STATE IN MEXICO

The story of the state of Texas and Coahuila or Coahuila y Tejas is interesting. Notice that Texas had two spellings in those days: Texas or Tejas. They were used equally often and were said alike (Tay'hăhs).

Remember, Mexico had gained her independence from Spain (in 1821). Then Iturbide had made himself emperor. He ruled very much like the Spanish had done before him, and the people did not like him either. After only two years (1823), a young general named Antonio Lopez de Santa Anna (Săn'tăh Ăh'năh) forced Iturbide out of Mexico and took over the government.

The following year (1824), Mexico set up a government something like that of the United States. Mexico was a republic, one nation with many states, which could elect a president. But Texas was not ready to be a state.

One reason that Texas was not ready to be a state was that it had very little money. The governor, Trespalacios, had tried to help by establishing a bank called "Banco Nacional de Tejas." The paper money this bank issued became no good when the new Mexican republic issued paper money too.

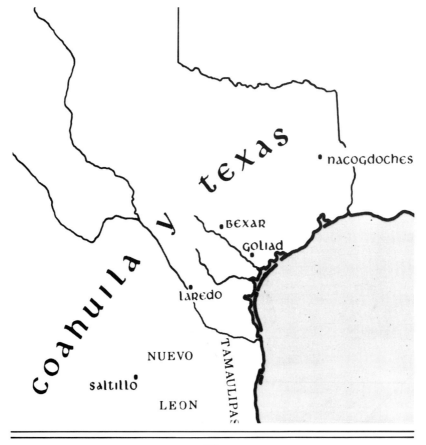

Texas had other problems. There was a problem in getting special papers for the settlers to show ownership of the land they were living on. There were problems with some Americans from the United States coming into east Texas to live without permission. Texas was still a very small frontier state at this time with only a few towns and not

many settlers. And there were no people who knew how to run the state government. The Spaniards who knew how to rule had left the state when it no longer belonged to Spain.

There were other frontier states with the same kind of problems. So in 1824, the states of Coahuila and Texas and Nuevo Leon decided to join together to form one big state. Before they could write the paper to do this, Nuevo Leon decided to take a chance and be a state all by itself. This left Coahuila and Texas to write up an agreement to become a state. This agreement was allowed by the Mexican Constitution of 1824.

The first governor of the new state of Coahuila y Tejas was Rafael Gonzáles (Gŏn′zǎ′lĕs) from San Antonio. He was elected by the people and served for four years. The Texas town of Gonzales was named for him in 1825.

The Constitution of 1824 was a very important document. It stated that when Texas had enough people and it was able to take care of its own problems, it could become a separate state again. This is important because, later, Texas did ask to become a separate state. When this request was ignored, it led to war.

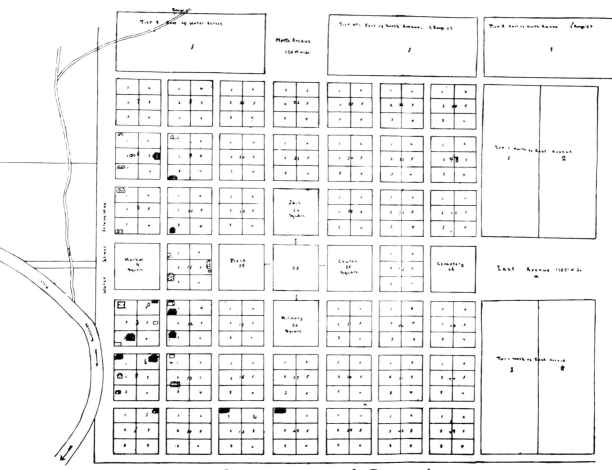

Inner town of Gonzales

THE "EJ" BRAND AND VICTORIA

One of the most famous Mexican men in early Texas was Martín de León (day'lay ōn'). He was from a wealthy *criollo* family, that is, a Spanish family that lived in Mexico. His family had planned to educate him in Europe, but de León chose a life of ranching and adventure.

He made a trip to Texas in 1805 and saw the beautiful grasslands, the flowing rivers and springs. He thought Texas was the best place for a ranch that he had ever seen and decided to move there.

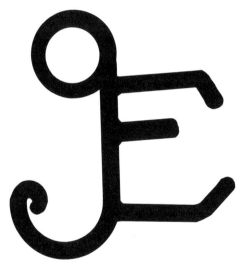

He developed a large cattle ranch on the Aransas River. He chose the "EJ" brand for his cattle, the oldest brand to be used in Texas. The "EJ" stood for "Espíritu Jesús," Spirit of Jesus. It had been used by a group of Catholic priests hundreds of years before.

Besides being a rancher, de León made an agreement with the new Mexican government (1824) to bring more Mexican families into Texas. Families who came to work and to build their homes in a new land were called colonists. De León helped the families to settle as a colony in the Guadalupe River valley. A town grew up there called Victoria. Victoria was named in honor of Mexico's first president, Guadalupe Victoria (pictured above).

GASPAR FLORES

When settlers from many parts of Mexico and the United States started coming to Texas to set up colonies, a man was needed to be in charge. He was called the commissioner of colonization. One commissioner (1826) was Gaspar Flores (Flōōr´ rĕs). His job was to decide where families could settle and how much land they could have. He could give out titles of land ownership or just let families live there for awhile.

There were many Indian tribes in Texas different from the Indians in Mexico that we read about earlier. One of the tribes in Texas was the Comanche Indians. They were well known for their love of fighting and were feared by settlers and other tribes. Flores was one of the few men in Texas who was able to talk with the Comanches. He was able to make peace agreements with them called treaties.

Flores was liked and respected by the Texans. He offered all his goods and cattle to the Texans who fought at the Alamo. Later, Flores was asked by the people to be one of the men to sign the Texas Declaration of Independence. He was on his way to sign this important paper when he died. His family had farms and ranches south of San Antonio. The town of Floresville is named in honor of this important family.

VERAMENDI AND BOWIE

Juan Martín de Veramendi (Va'răh měn'dě) of San Antonio was elected mayor of his city in 1824. He served well for six years. Then he was elected vice-governor of the state of Coahuila y Tejas (1830). The vice-governor is next in line to be governor if something happens to the governor. Veramendi had to go to Mexico City to accept this office in person. On the way to Mexico City, he met an Anglo American named James Bowie. Bowie was a famous knife-fighter who came to Texas look-

ing for adventure. They became good friends and traveled back to San Antonio together. Veramendi invited Bowie to visit his home and meet his family. Bowie fell in love with Ursula Veramendi, his oldest daughter. She was

described as "a very beautiful woman." Soon Bowie and Ursula were married.

Both families moved to Saltillo, the capital of Coahuila y Tejas. Here Veramendi worked with the state government. Bowie purchased machinery in the United States for making cotton into cloth and brought it to Saltillo. There, Veramendi and Bowie went into the cotton mill business together (1831).

After a short time, the governor, José

María Letona, died, and Veramendi became governor. In the summer of 1833, the dreaded disease of cholera began to take many lives. Veramendi decided to take the two families to his summer home in Monclova, hoping to escape the disease. But Veramendi and most of his family, including Bowie's wife and two children, died from cholera that summer. Bowie did not get cholera because he was on a business trip to the United States. He was very sad about the deaths of his family. Bowie gave up the cotton mill and left Saltillo. After this, he spent most of his time fighting Indians and exploring new land in Texas.

A FIGHTER WHO LOST HIS HOME

Many of the families that de León brought to Texas became ranchers. Some of them worked at other jobs. Placido Benavides (Bĕn´ ăh vēē´dĕs) was one of these.

Benavides came to Texas as a bookkeeper for the colony started by de León. He married one of de León's daughters, Augustina de León. They were given a ranch on Placido Creek and some land in Victoria. In the center of town, they built a large home of logs which they named Round Top House. It was built like a fort and had small openings in the walls to shoot through. During the Indian raids, the colonists came to Round Top House for safety.

Benavides was liked by the people and was elected mayor of Victoria in 1832. Benavides also did a great deal to help Texas

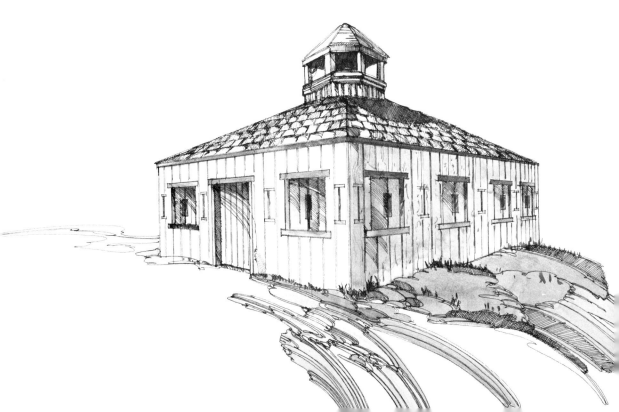

gain her independence from Mexico. He was the leader of a group of Mexican Texan ranchers from around Victoria. The ranchers left their homes to help other Texans fight for their freedom (1835-36). When they returned, they found many of their homes and ranches had been taken over by settlers from the United States. This happened to Benavides. The new settlers had found the homes empty and had moved in to stay. They would not leave. Benavides was angry because the government would not make them leave the property. He had no home in Texas any more, so he moved his family to Louisiana. He lived there until his death in 1837.

THE TEXAS DECLARATION OF INDEPENDENCE

Earlier in this book, you read about Mexico gaining her independence from Spain (1821). As a new free country, Mexico first had an emperor for two years (1821-1823), then General Santa Anna controlled the government for one year. Finally, they set up a

government like that of the United States (1824) and elected a president. There were states in this new republic, and Texas became a state with Coahuila, named Coahuila y Tejas.

In Coahuila y Tejas, as in other states, people argued about the best way to make decisions and run the new country. Some people liked the Constitution of 1824, which promised that everyone would have the same rights and could tell the government what to do. People who thought this way were called Federalists. Others thought the nation should have one man who had all the power and would tell the people what he wanted them to do. People who thought this way were called Centralists. The man who thought he should rule was Santa Anna.

Most of the people who lived in Texas were Federalists. They did not want Santa Anna or any one powerful man to be a ruler. The Texans decided to hold a meeting at a place called Washington-on-the-Brazos and talk about who should rule them. Among others, seven Mexican Texans were elected by the people to go to the meeting and talk for them. Only three of these men actually were able to attend.

The people at the meeting spent many hours talking and thinking. They had to decide if Texas should fight to become a separate state from Coahuila again, or if they should fight to become a nation, completely free from Mexican rule.

They remembered the letters they had sent to Mexico City. The letters asked the president of Mexico to let Coahuila y Tejas divide and become separate states again. The letters had not even been answered! If they wanted to be a separate state, they would surely have to fight the government in order to do so.

They thought about what it would be like to remain as a state in Mexico. They would surely be ruled by one powerful man from Mexico City. They did not like that idea. That was almost as bad as being ruled by Spain!

The men decided Texas should fight for independence from Mexico. They wanted Texas to be a free nation where Texans could make all the decisions for themselves.

On March 2, 1836, the three Mexican Texans and 56 others signed Texas's Declaration of Independence. The Mexican signers were José Antonio Navarro, José Francisco Ruiz and Lorenzo de Zavala. By signing this paper, the men let all people know that Texas was now fighting Mexico to become a free nation.

NAVARRO AND THE LEG IRONS

José Antonio Navarro (Nă văr′rōw) was one of the signers of the Texas Declaration of Independence in 1836. But he was known for many other things as well. He had taken part in everything important that had happened in Texas for many years.

Navarro was born in San Antonio in 1795. He took part in the events which freed Mexico from Spain. When Gutiérrez captured the cities of Nacogdoches, La Bahía and San

Antonio, Navarro was actively helping. When Gutiérrez lost his command to Toledo, and Toledo lost the war to Spain, Navarro had to hide in Louisiana for three years. Later he was forgiven, and he returned to Texas.

He served in the state government for a number of years and became friends with Stephen F. Austin. It was while serving in office that Navarro wrote a law which gave land to Texas families. The law gave a special amount of land to any family who would build a home on it and plant crops. In later years this kind of law would be called "the homestead law." In 1836, Navarro was elected to represent San Antonio in the meeting at Washington-on-the-Brazos. There he signed

the Declaration of Independence and helped to write the Texas Constitution giving new laws for the Texas Republic.

Five years later, Navarro went on a trip to Santa Fe with a group of men who were trying to make New Mexico a part of Texas. He was captured, spent four years in a Mexican jail and escaped while still wearing leg irons. When he got back to Texas, he added a line and a circle to the brand of his ranch. This showed the leg irons he wore while a prisoner in Mexico suffering for his country.

He spent the rest of his life in government service to Texas. Navarro County in Texas is named in his honor. Its county seat, Corsicana, is named for his father's birthplace, the island of Corsica.

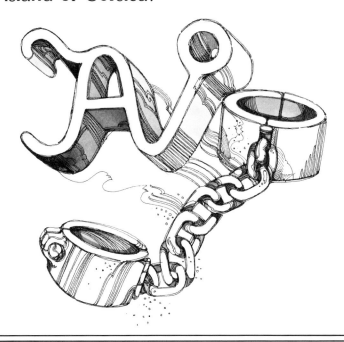

RUIZ AND THE INDIANS

Another signer of Texas's Declaration of Independence was José Francisco Ruiz (Rōō ēēs'), an uncle of Navarro. He, too, was a San Antonian (born in 1780). His parents wanted him to have a good education, so they sent him to Spain while he was still a boy. He liked school and learned to be a teacher.

When he returned to Texas in 1803, he was full of ideas. He thought people should make their own rules and laws. He believed decisions about money, schools, taxes, roads and everything else should come from the people. He had many friends who listened to his ideas and agreed with him.

When the war between Mexico and Spain started, he and Navarro joined the army of Gutiérrez (1813). When the army lost the battle at the Medina River, a few men escaped to the United States. But not Ruiz! Ruiz escaped but went to live among the Indians. He remained with them about eight years until Mexico gained its independence.

After he returned to San Antonio, Ruiz became a colonel in the Mexican army. He had learned a great deal about the Indians during his stay with them. He used this knowledge to help him serve the army and his country.

After signing the Texas Declaration of Independence, Ruiz was the first senator from San Antonio in the new Texas government.

DE ZAVALA AND THE TEXAS FLAG

An Indian from Yucatán, a state in Mexico, was another signer of the Texas Declaration of Independence in 1836. His name was Lorenzo de Zavala (dāy′Sǎ vǎ′lǎ). He did many important things before coming to Texas in 1835.

For one thing, he was sent by the people of Yucatán to speak for them, to be their representative, in Spain. He then served in the

Mexican government (1822) and made many suggestions about changes that should be made. He was elected as governor of a state in Mexico in 1827. Later, de Zavala became head of the Mexican Treasury and was trusted with the nation's money. Also, he was given a grant of land on which to settle families in Texas. Some land would be given to each family who settled in Texas, and some to de Zavala for bringing the families there.

When Santa Anna was in power, de Zavala was chosen to go to France to represent his country (1833). When he returned from France, he left the Mexican government and moved his family to Texas (1835). He built their home outside of Harrisburg near the present city of Houston.

After signing the Texas Declaration of Independence, he was named vice-president of the new Republic of Texas, serving only until someone could be elected by the people. Shortly thereafter, he designed the first official flag for the Republic of Texas. It looked different from the Texas flag of today. It was blue with a single gold star and T - E - X - A - S written around it.

While serving as vice-president, he became too ill to work. He left his office to be at home. One day, he and his son went for a ride in their boat on Buffalo Bayou. The boat turned over, and de Zavala saved his son from drowning. But de Zavala was already sick and weak before this happened. He took a fever, and in three days he died. He had spent his entire life helping others, and in the end, he lost his life because he had saved his son.

Brother Against Brother

There were many Mexican Texans who fought and died for Texas independence. Gregorio Esparza (Āys pár'sǎ) was one of them. Esparza was one of the first to volunteer to fight. He had joined the Texans who believed that people should vote and decide things for themselves. People who believed this way were called Federalists.

The Federalists decided to fight the Mexican army in San Antonio because the soldiers believed another way and were Centralists. The Centralists believed that one powerful man should rule the country and tell everyone else what to do. Santa Anna was the head of the Centralist group. He had sent his brother-in-law, General Cós, to San Antonio as commander of the Mexican army.

After bitter fighting in town, General Cós lost many men and agreed to surrender (1835). Cós and his men who were not Texans were told to leave and never return. One of the soldiers with Cós was Gregorio Esparza's brother, Francisco. Since Francisco was a Texan, he was allowed to stay only after he agreed not to fight any more.

Here were two brothers who loved each other very much but did not think alike. When war came, they found they were not on the same side. This happens sometimes when people believe in different things, and it can cause a man to fight his brother.

ENRIQUE — A BOY AT THE ALAMO

In San Antonio, there was excitement in the air. Enrique, the eight-year-old son of Gregorio Esparza, felt the excitement, too, but he was also a little frightened. He had heard that Santa Anna with his huge army was coming to town.

It had been an insult to Santa Anna's power to have his brother-in-law driven out of Texas. This had made him very angry, and he wanted to return to Texas with his army and personally crush the rebelling Texans.

Enrique remembered how his father had fought General Cós three months before. He also remembered that his uncle Francisco had

been one of the soldiers with General Cós. Uncle Francisco had been told to be ready if Santa Anna needed him later.

Suddenly, a messenger rode into town shouting, "Santa Anna is coming! His army has just been seen outside of town." A crowd gathered around him, and he continued, "Santa Anna will fight until every Federalist soldier in Texas is dead or captured!" Enrique wondered what would happen next.

His mother, Mrs. Esparza, was worried. "Why doesn't the wagon get here to take us away from here? I have everything packed and ready to go."

"We must move quickly," his father, Gregorio, thought. "It is getting dark, and the wagon may not come in time. I must join the other Texans in the Alamo to man a cannon."

Gregorio said to his wife, "Quickly, bring the food and a few clothes. We will take the children and go to the Alamo together."

As it grew darker, the Esparzas and their four young children slipped quietly out of their home and made their way to the Alamo.

When they arrived, however, they found the huge, heavy doors closed and barred.

"What shall we do?" asked Mrs. Esparza. "We cannot take the children back home tonight. It would not be safe there now."

"I will help, mamá," said Enrique. He pounded on the doors with his small fist. Gregorio called to the guard standing on the

wall. The guard recognized Gregorio and his family. Soon all the Esparzas were lifted over the wall and raised through a window into the Alamo. Enrique bumped into a cannon in the dark and wondered if it would be one his father might fire. They were now safe inside the Alamo, at least for this night!

In the morning, Enrique could hardly wait to explore his new home. The Texans were using the old mission as a fort. The old buildings and stone walls had been repaired, and there were cannons mounted on top of some of them. The Alamo looked like an interesting place in which to play. "It will be a real adventure to be here," Enrique thought to himself.

It was not long before Santa Anna's soldiers reached the Alamo and began the fight that would be remembered by all Texans. Gregorio joined the other men in the Alamo who were fighting. Some were Mexican Texans, some were Anglo Americans, but they were on the same side because they believed the same way about government.

Santa Anna's cannons were fired at them day and night. There was little time for sleeping or eating. They took turns for a little rest or a quick bite of food and then went right back to their posts.

Enrique soon realized there would be little time for play. He had to do what he could to help his father and the others. Early one morning, he took his father some food and saw that he was very tired. "Papá, why don't you stop and rest? I am afraid for you," he said. "You are very brave, but I am afraid you will get hurt or be killed."

Esparza looked at his son with love in his eyes. "I am not afraid to die, Enrique, if it means that you and the others will be free. I will try to be careful, but if I am killed, I want you to be brave. Take care of your mother for me. Help her with the little ones. You must be

the man in the family if anything happens to me." He held his son close and kissed him.

Enrique hugged his father. "I will, papá," he promised. "I am proud of you." Enrique ran back to be with the women and other children.

Gregorio turned to the small cannon and began to fire it. The battle grew worse. They had been surrounded by the enemy for 13

days, and the enemy far outnumbered them.

The defenders of the Alamo fought bravely, but on March 6, 1836, the Mexican troops broke into the fort. Santa Anna had given orders that none of the defenders would be spared. All were to be killed.

When the battle was over, Santa Anna had won, and the men who had fought in the Alamo were dead. Esparza's body was found slumped over his cannon, with a bullet in his chest and a sword slash in his side. It was the day before his thirty-fourth birthday. Enrique remembered his father's request and helped his mother. The five Esparzas and about eight others were the only ones who had survived the Battle of the Alamo. It was a very sad time in Texas.

Santa Anna ordered his soldiers to gather up all the bodies of the Alamo defenders and burn them. This was one way to show the Texans who ruled the country. He could keep the dead men from getting a proper funeral and Christian burial.

Francisco, who was on Santa Anna's side, felt very sad about his brother Gregorio's death. He did not want Gregorio's body to be

burned. So he went to Santa Anna and asked a special favor. He asked for the body of his brother so he could give it a proper burial. Santa Anna allowed him to take Gregorio's body so the family could have a funeral. It was the only one of the bodies from the Alamo that was not burned after the battle.

Enrique Esparza lived to be 89 years old. He was always proud of his father who had fought and died at the Alamo. He taught his own family to feel that way, too. When Enrique died, his family said on his death announcement, "The deceased was a son of one of the soldiers on the side of the Americans in the Battle of the Alamo."

A WOMAN FROM THE ALAMO

One of the most famous women in Texas history is Señora Andrea Castonon Ramirez Candalaria (Căn′dă lă′rē ăh). It is said that she was one of the women who survived the Battle of the Alamo. She lived to be 113 years old! The story of her life is fascinating.

Madame Candalaria was born in Nuevo Laredo, Mexico, in 1785; but when she was three years old, she moved to Laredo, Texas, with her parents. Her father was Spanish, and her mother was Mexican.

Madame Candalaria was 25 years old when she moved to San Antonio. San Antonio was a very small town then. Many families lived in adobe houses. She watched San Antonio grow into a very large town with many people. Much of her life was spent in helping people in trouble and nursing those who were sick. Madame Candalaria's help was welcome during the smallpox epidemics, when this deadly disease spread quickly from one person to another.

During her life in San Antonio, many interesting events took place. One of the stories she told was about Santa Anna. She said that a short time before the Battle of the Alamo she saw Santa Anna, the Mexican general, ride into the city disguised as a farmer. He drove a mule and pretended to sell hay from his wagon. But what he was really doing was mapping out the city and making plans for the battle. It was her idea that General Santa Anna did not want to trust this important job to one of his men. He did it himself.

Madame Candalaria said she was also present at the Alamo during the battle. She did not say when she went to the Alamo or how she got there. She did say, however, that she helped take care of the wounded men. She said that she had nursed James Bowie, when he became ill during the battle. According to her story, Bowie died of pneumonia the day before the Alamo was captured.

When the Mexican soldiers stormed inside and were killing all the Texans who were not already dead, she threw herself upon Bowie's body. She told them he had died of a disease and not from one of their bullets. Because of this, she did not think his body should be burned with the others. She pleaded for his body to be given to her so she might give it a regular burial.

Some of Santa Anna's soldiers thought Bowie might really be alive and was just "playing dead" to trick them into letting him escape. While she was pleading, Madame Candalaria said, one of the Mexican soldiers drew his sword and thrust it through Bowie's side, wounding her on the chin and right wrist at the same time. She carried scars of two such

wounds to her grave. After she had been silenced, Bowie's body was taken out by the soldiers. It was placed on the pile of bodies and burned along with more than 180 others who had died defending the Alamo. Madame Candalaria was one of the 13 women and children who were not massacred by the Mexican soldiers.

Many of the women who had helped the Texans were forced to work hard by the Mexican soldiers as punishment. Madame Candalaria was one of them. She was soon set free, but she did not say how this happened.

During her lifetime, Madame Candalaria had four children of her own. She adopted 22 orphan children to rear as well. She was known as one of the best cooks of Mexican food in Texas. She made much money cooking suppers for famous and rich people. Most of her money was used to help the poor and care for the needy.

In her old age, she lived in a small home in San Antonio with one of her daughters. She had a good memory, and many people came to ask about things that had happened when she was young. She was the oldest living person in Texas at that time who had lived through the Battle of the Alamo. When she was 106 years old (1891), the Texas government voted to give her a check for $12 each month. It was for her services at the Alamo and for her nursing the smallpox patients in San Antonio.

PANCHITA, "THE ANGEL OF GOLIAD"

During the time that Texas was fighting Mexico to become a free land, many people were killed. In the midst of all this conflict and violence, however, there were people who were interested in saving lives. One of these was Francisca Alavéz. Some called her Francita Alvarez. But soon she was best known to everyone by her nickname "Panchita – the Angel of Goliad."

Panchita was the wife of Captain Telesforo Alavéz, an officer in the Mexican army. He served as paymaster most of the time, but sometimes he had to fight in the bloody battles against the Texans. He was a soldier and had to do what he was ordered to do. This did not mean that he always liked what his orders told him to do. He agreed with his wife, Panchita, when she said "I do not like killing people."

Panchita decided to help the Texans who became prisoners whenever she could. In San Patricio, a small town in Texas, a Texan named Reuben Brown was taken prisoner during a battle. He was scheduled to be shot by the Mexican troops commanded by General Urrea. Panchita found out about the execution that was planned. She and a priest went to the general to plead for the prisoner's life. General Urrea agreed to their request. Later the prisoner was able to escape.

Another time, at the Texas port of Copano, William Miller and 75 of his men were captured by soldiers under the command of Panchita's husband. The hands and feet of the prisoners were tied so tightly that the blood almost stopped circulating. Panchita begged her husband to loosen the ropes, and he yielded to her plea. Her concern saved their lives. Later, with her help, they were able to escape. Many years later, Panchita received a letter from Colonel Miller thanking her for her life-saving kindness to him and his men.

A very important event in her life happened at Goliad. A group of Texas soldiers commanded by Colonel Fannin were captured and brought to Goliad. Many were sick and wounded. They were told they would be put on a ship and returned to the United States. One night Captain Alavéz looked worried and

paced the floor.

"What is wrong?" said Panchita. "What is bothering you? Tell me so I can help."

"My dear," he said, "how I wish you could. The men who are singing in the prison expect to go home tomorrow. But General Urrea has just received a command that they must be shot instead!"

"But, husband!" she exclaimed. "Tomorrow is Palm Sunday! Who would do such a thing on a Holy Day?"

"My general has received the command from Santa Anna, and he has just ordered me to shoot the men. How I hate the job of being a soldier. But I know what I must do," he said to her sadly.

Panchita thought for a moment, then whispered to herself, "He knows what he must do, and I know what I must do." She was

thinking that many of those captured were young men. They had their entire lives ahead of them, and she wanted to save as many as she could.

It was a long restless night for both of them. Early in the morning, before the sun came up, Panchita went to her friend, the wife of General Urrea. She asked for help in saving some of the prisoners. Lady Urrea agreed to do what she could.

As General Urrea's officers were marching some of the prisoners out to the field to be shot, Panchita and Lady Urrea saw a young boy among them. They went quickly to the officers and begged to have the boy released in their care. They succeeded in saving his life. Later, the 15-year-old boy was helped to escape. He was Benjamin Hughes from Kentucky and lived to be 60 years old. When he died, he left papers telling the story and praising the mercy of "the Angel, Panchita."

Shortly after saving the boy, Panchita heard the soldiers marching more prisoners out to be shot. As they marched by, she was able to slip several of the young men from the group when the guards were not looking. She hid them in her tent until after the slaughter had taken place. She gave them food and bandaged their wounds. Later she helped them to escape.

"You are the 'Angel of Goliad,' " they said. And that became her name.

FATHER AND SON FOR TEXAS — THE SEGUÍNS

Some Mexican Texans did more than others to help Texas become a better place in which to live. Erasmo Seguín (Say geen') was one of them. He set up one of the first schools owned by the town of San Antonio, the city where he was born. He tried new ways of growing cotton on his land. At one time, he served as mayor of San Antonio; and at another time, he was the postmaster.

When General Cós and his Mexican soldiers came to Texas, Seguín wanted to be their friend. But the soldiers were unfriendly to him, and Seguín changed his mind. He decided to be friends only with Texans. He sent many wagons full of food to the Texans who were fighting for independence. He also gave them horses and mules from his ranch.

The Texans liked Seguín and the things he did to help them. They elected him to go to the special meeting to talk about Texas independence – the Convention of 1836. He wanted to go but was unable to attend. Seguín spent his whole life helping his fellow man and his state.

Erasmo Seguín had a son named Juan who followed in his father's footsteps in helping Texas. He was one of the first to warn Texans that Santa Anna was no longer their friend. Juan spent long hours getting Mexican Texans to join a group to fight the Centralist army. His company was made up entirely of Mexican Texans. Under Juan's command, they served Texas well and bravely.

Juan was one of the few Texans who fought at both the Alamo and at San Jacinto. He and his company went to help Colonel William B. Travis at the Alamo. Colonel Travis decided to send a message to Colonel Fannin at Goliad asking for help. Juan was asked to carry the message because he spoke Spanish and knew the countryside. He left his troops at the Alamo and rode through enemy lines to deliver the message. On the way back, he learned the Alamo had already been captured and all the soldiers killed. Seven of the nine Mexican Texans who died in the Alamo were

Seguín's men.

Juan joined General Sam Houston's army at Gonzales and soon formed another volunteer group of ranchers made up entirely of Mexican Texans. It was a cavalry unit; that is, a unit in which the soldiers rode horses. This company served as scouts in Houston's army

and as a fighting unit at San Jacinto. Most of the men spoke only Spanish. One of the men, who could speak both English and Spanish, was José Antonio Menchaca (Měn chǎ′ kǎ). Menchaca acted as an interpreter for those who did not understand English.

As the Battle of San Jacinto drew near,

General Houston asked Seguín's company of Mexican Texans to stay behind and guard the horses and equipment. Perhaps Houston was afraid the Mexican Texans might be mistaken for the enemy and shot by mistake. Nevertheless, Seguín and his men were insulted by Houston's suggestion. Menchaca spoke for Seguín and the company. "We joined the army

to fight for freedom. We are prepared to face the enemy, and we will die if we must. We did not join the army to herd horses or watch equipment. If you do not want our help in fighting, we will return to our families. They need our help in going to Louisiana for safety. That would be better than tending horses!"

General Houston was convinced that they

wanted to fight. He changed his mind and let them join the other soldiers. They fought bravely at San Jacinto and helped drive the Mexican army out of Texas.

Seguín stayed in the army and later was sent back to San Antonio as a military commander. One of the things he did was to gather the ashes of the Alamo defenders who had been burned. He buried them with full military honors at San Fernando Cathedral in San Antonio. The funeral address was delivered by Juan Seguín in Spanish.

Seguín was well liked by the people. He was elected to the Texas government and also became mayor of San Antonio in 1841. The town of Walnut Springs changed its name to Seguin to honor him and his father.

Seguín, however, was not always honored by Texans. On a trip to Mexico, he

discovered that the Mexican government was planning to send their army back to take San Antonio from the Texans. Seguín warned the people and the Texas government. The people thought this would not happen and did not get ready to fight. When the Mexican army arrived in March 1842, they captured San Antonio easily. The Mexican commander spread the lie that Juan Seguín had helped him. This story made some people wonder if Seguín was still a friend to Texas.

The Mexican army left San Antonio after only two days when they heard the Texan army was coming. But even after they left, many people still believed the lie about Juan Seguín. They blamed Seguín for many of the other troubles in San Antonio and said they would kill him. Seguín left for Laredo.

When he arrived in Laredo, he was arrested by the Mexicans and put in jail. He

was given a choice by Santa Anna. He was told he could spend the rest of his life in jail or he could join the Mexican army as a major. He would have to fight the Texans who had once been his friends. Seguín made his decision and agreed to join their army.

The Mexican army planned a second invasion of Texas in September, 1842, and now Seguín returned to San Antonio as a member of the Mexican army. He fought in several battles. While in San Antonio, Seguín learned that his ranch had been sold by the government for taxes.

After the Mexican army was beaten at the Battle of Salado, they decided to return to Mexico. Seguín returned with them, taking his family and others who wanted to go.

He was made a colonel in the Mexican army and took part in many other famous Mexican battles. Later he left the Mexican army and was allowed to return to Texas.

Seguín spent the rest of his life living sometimes in Texas and sometimes in Mexico. He died in Nuevo Laredo in 1890 and was buried there.

In 1969, some citizens of Seguin, Texas, visited his grave in Mexico to honor him. They wanted to have his body moved to the Texas city that was named for him. During the Bicentennial Celebration of the United States in 1976, his body was reburied in Seguin as a Texas hero.

POSTSCRIPT FOR VOLUME ONE

In this volume, we have looked at some of the stories from the beginning of Mexico to the time of Texas independence. But this is not the end of the Mexican story. It is only a stopping place, the end of Volume One. Volume Two begins where this volume ends and includes stories of warriors, outlaws, ranchers and workers, settlers and citizens. It continues the story of the Mexican Texans up to today.

The stories you have just read are only about a few of those who have helped make Texas what it is today. There are many other people who have done interesting things and have equally interesting stories to share. Possibly your parents, grandparents or someone else in your family could tell you about some of them. You might like to record some of these stories and begin your own personal or family history.

The stories included in this volume show how life was in the early days and how people tried to solve their problems. Some stories remind us that life has always had difficulties. Perhaps, also, you will see that *one person* can make a difference . . . to his neighborhood, to his state and to his country. Perhaps you could be that kind of person someday!

PHOTO CREDITS

p. 9   Library of Congress, Washington, D.C.

p. 10   Cubas, Antonio Garcia. *The Republic of Mexico in 1876.*
        Mexico, D.F., 1876.

p. 10   Michaud y Thomas, Julio. *Album Pintoresco de la
        Republica Mexicana.* Mexico: Julio Michaud y Thomas,
        n.d. (about 1848).

p. 14   Cass, Alfonso. *The Aztecs.* Norman: University of
        Oklahoma Press, 1958, p. 91.

p. 16   The University of Texas Barker Texas History Center,
        Austin, Texas.

p. 17   Museo Nacional de Antropologia, Mexico, D.F.

p. 18   Series of illustrations on folk heroes. Mexico, D.F.:
        Kleenex, S.A.

p. 26   *Harper's New Monthly Magazine,* Vol. 12. New York:
        Harper and Bros., 1855, p. 19.

p. 31   *Harper's New Monthly Magazine,* Vol. 12. New York:
        Harper and Bros., 1855, p. 16.

p. 37   Riva-Palacio, D. Vicente. *Mexico, a Traves de los Siglos,*
        Vol. 3. Mexico: Ballasca y Comp., 1887-1888, p. 22.

p. 39   Castenada, Carlos E. *Our Catholic Heritage in Texas,
        1519-1936.* Austin: Von Boeckmann-Jones Co., 1936.

p. 40   The Institute of Texan Cultures.

p. 41   The Institute of Texan Cultures.

p. 43   Nick Sanchez Collection, Mrs. Yolanda Parker, Laredo.

p. 44   Thompson, Jerry. *Sabers on the Rio Grande.* Austin:
        Presidial Press, 1974, p. 12.

p. 45   The Institute of Texan Cultures.

p. 46   Lossing, Benson G. *Centennial Edition of the History of
        the U.S.A.* Hartford: Thomas Belknap, 1876, p. 83.

p. 47   *Harper's Weekly,* Nov. 21, 1868, pp. 741-42.

p. 48   The Institute of Texan Cultures.

p. 55   Cadena, Longinos. *Elementos de Historia General de
        Historia Patria.* Mexico: Herrero Hermanos Sucesores,
        1922, p. 94.

p. 56   Michaud y Thomas, Julio. *Album Pintoresco de la
        Republica Mexicana.* Mexico: Julio Michaud y Thomas,
        n.d. (about 1848).

p. 57   Michaud y Thomas, Julio. *Album Pintoresco de la
        Republica Mexicana.* Mexico: Julio Michaud y Thomas,
        n.d. (about 1848).

p. 58   Orozco, Jose Clemente. Mural, Government Palace,
        Guadalajara. "Hidalgo y La Ruta de la Independencia."
        Artes de Mexico, No. 122, Año XVI, 1969, p. 86.

p. 59   "Cronica del Traje Militar en Mexico de Siglo XVI al XX."
        Artes de Mexico, No. 102, Año XV, 1968.

p. 60   The Institute of Texan Cultures.

p. 62   The Institute of Texan Cultures.

p. 65   The Institute of Texan Cultures.

p. 66   "Cronica del Traje Militar en Mexico de Siglo XVI al XX." *Artes de Mexico,* No. 102, Año XV, 1968.

p. 67   Museum of History, Castillo de Chapultepec, Mexico, D.F.

p. 68   *The San Antonio Light* Collection, The Institute of Texan Cultures.

p. 69   Texas State Library, Austin, Texas.

p. 70   The Institute of Texan Cultures.

p. 73   *The Quarterly of the Texas State Historical Association,* Vol. VIII. Austin, Texas, 1905.

p. 74   Jim de Leon, Victoria, Texas.

p. 75   San Jacinto Museum of History, Deer Park, Texas.

p. 77   The University of Texas Humanities Research Center, Austin, Texas.

p. 79   Texas State Capitol, Austin, Texas.

p. 80   The Library of the Daughters of the Republic of Texas at the Alamo, San Antonio, Texas.

p. 83   Grimes, Roy. *300 Years in Victoria County.* Victoria: The Victoria Advocate Publishing Co., 1968, p. 108.

p. 84   The Institute of Texan Cultures.

p. 85   Museum of History, Castillo de Chapultepec, Mexico, D.F.

p. 87   Mrs. Artie Davis, Navasota, Texas.

p. 88   The Library of the Daughters of the Republic of Texas at the Alamo, San Antonio, Texas.

p. 89   Estate of Randy Steffen, Cisco, Texas.

p. 91   Texas State Historical Association, Austin, Texas.

p. 92   No source.

p. 93   Charton, Edouard, ed. *Le Tour du Monde,* Vol. I. Paris: Hachette et Cie, 1860, p. 349.

p. 94   Senate Chamber, Texas State Capitol, Austin, Texas.

p. 95   Louis Lenz, Houston, Texas.

p. 96   The University of Texas Barker Texas History Center, Austin, Texas.

p. 104   The Library of the Daughters of the Republic of Texas at the Alamo, San Antonio, Texas.

p. 107   San Antonio Conservation Society, San Antonio, Texas.

p. 112   Texas State Library, Austin, Texas.

p. 113   Texas State Library, Austin, Texas.

p. 115   Texas State Library, Austin, Texas.

p. 117   Texas State Capitol, Austin, Texas.

p. 118   The Library of the Daughters of the Republic of Texas at the Alamo, San Antonio, Texas.

p. 119   *The San Antonio Light* Collection, The Institute of Texan Cultures.